QUIET TREE

poems by

DM Frech

Finishing Line Press
Georgetown, Kentucky

QUIET TREE

Copyright © 2023 by DM Frech
ISBN 979-8-88838-363-6 First Edition
All rights reserved under International and Pan-American Copyright Conventions. No part of this book may be reproduced in any manner whatsoever without written permission from the publisher, except in the case of brief quotations embodied in critical articles and reviews.

ACKNOWLEDGMENTS

DM Frech has published in *Writer's Journal*, *The International Library of Poetry*, *The Poets Choice*, *Noble House*, *WayWords Literary Journal* and *The Journal of The Writers Guild of Virginia*. She's won several awards in non-fiction from Hampton Roads Writers and her photography can be found on *Streetlight Magazine*'s website and *New Feathers Anthology*.

Many thanks to Finishing Line Press for publishing her first chapbook, *Words From Walls* and her second chapbook, *Quiet Tree*. And thank you Jesus.

Publisher: Leah Huete de Maines
Editor: Christen Kincaid
Cover Art: DM Frech
Author Photo: DM Frech
Cover Design: Elizabeth Maines McCleavy

Order online: www.finishinglinepress.com
also available on amazon.com

Author inquiries and mail orders:
Finishing Line Press
PO Box 1626
Georgetown, Kentucky 40324
USA

Table of Contents

Darken Day 1
Death Waits 2
Dying Shame 3
Forgotten 4
God Save The Weak 5
A Clearing in His Shadows 6
Jesus Woke Me 7
Like Stars 8
Lost You 9
Love Poem 10
Memory 11
My Sixty Second Stroke 12
Noted 13
Ocean Waves 14
Of Flesh 15
Passage 16
Prison 17
Priviliage 18
Quiet Tree 19
Slain Dreams 20
The Night Is Not My Friend 21
We Love 22
We Should Not Talk 23
What Becomes Of 24
Wish 25
Wonderful Moments 26
Writing 27
Your Grace 28
You Want the Truth 29

For Andrew & Samuel Frech, my sons and greatest joy who inspire me daily to leave the swamp and climb the mountain

And to my dad, Steven Kasmauski, who loved unconditionally

DARKEN DAY

Darken day
the way you stood
seem to say
you were
full of grief

nothing left
around
was found,
only pity

for your brief
sweeten hand
upon my chest
before I rest

while you slept
while night
grey and foggy

covered flowers
cards and gifts

meant to soften
the news of death.

DEATH WAITS

Dark and dreary we sit
in our rooms, wait to churn
voices that loom over our heads
for verdicts we try to flee
none could stop, or change
or conceive that death waits
in our destiny.

DYING SHAME

Coffin
up from sleep
down in the dumps
the rebel
lay in his coffin
where none came to look
none came to speak
for this man
this unknown
reflection
of a trodden life
crushed and destroyed
where winds blow
his presence cold
was someone's son
was a baby once
now
unknown
unknown.

FORGOTTEN

Amidst a rambling thought
one clear word, forgotten.
Confronted with doubt and fear
a message arrived
by years of misunderstood choices.

Forgotten.

All had been or nearly all
plowed by daydreaming,
scenes of lovely thoughts
cast their vote,
dispel the sting.

The past forgotten
by means of distractions,
where time rest, memories
flounder in moments gone.

It would be forgotten,
this voyage, my life,
why should I care
to leave nothing.

There is something,
haunting,
in being
forgotten.

GOD SAVE THE WEAK

God save the weak
those who cower in shadows
and darken crevices,
afraid to walk in the day,
they creep at night.
God full of mercy send help,
to keep those falling
from being shred
let all be saved in grace
let all rest in peace
in loving hands
in a kind and generous embrace
its only goal to convince
the good to speak
to calm the torrent beast.

A CLEARING IN HIS SHADOWS
for Ken

Pain was born
suddenly in grief
from his death . . .
in the dead of winter
in the coldest month,
he was forty-nine
when he failed
his heart stopped
his mind froze
his body lay
curled like a child,
seeking a reprieve
a comfort in self.

In darkness he arrived
to a clearing in his shadows
past melancholy, past battles
to peace, eternal peace.

He would see
what made his life
the gift it was
not the ghost he fought
it would be the breath
he needed, the clearing
he always sought.

JESUS WOKE ME

Jesus woke me from my grave
to say, He did save and would again
as often as day makes day
as often as sea meets shore
as birds fly south, as we war
Jesus would save to give me
hope, vigor, and peace
lift my burden, foster relief
days to glory shine in light
furnish love in darkest night.

LIKE STARS

God said,
you are like stars
in the night sky
that slay the dark

bright you shine
to let shadows know
you light the path
for the lost and weary
for those who need
to quench their thirst
for those who seek
a star, to guide
their weary soul,
save their broken heart

you are like stars
bright you shine
in the night sky
to slay the dark.

LOST YOU
Published in The International Library of Poetry

Passing through I saw you
wandering in my mind
where I could find you
as I pleased
and it was good.

But I miss you still
in the darkness
where I can see nothing
but my empty heart.

LOVE POEM

As though we have always been
As though day and night had blend
As though our birth exist eternal.
Love, our love
soft like dew, comfort too
like rest when work is done
our love set in sun
brought joy in rain
gave birth in death
we, you, and us
run as though we flew
nothing more could do
what God had made
none could undo.

MEMORY

Memory
suffocates
one cannot move
only recall

frozen action
in time, past
decisions made today
do not change
yesterday

events that made our lives
make us now, mine and me
a person I call myself,

memories

live in figments
stir our hollow void
disrupt events
destroy our joy

we should take
those memories
hide them
in our head
to wander
aimless
until dead.

MY SIXTY SECOND STROKE

The weak
fell
could not
be lifted
around the frail
the strong
held
until
all was good
where footing
failed
we stood
to say
God was on our side
today.

NOTED

Wanted
to say
good-bye
but
no one
to tell,
no one would
notice
I had
left.

Wanted
to say
all is well
but who
to whisper
my secret,
sit up,
note
me
gone.

In my heart
I breathed
my last
good-bye.
It lasted
long enough
to see that
I had departed
and it was
noted
by me.

OCEAN WAVES

Ocean waves
a place to dive
a place to sink
to the bottom
to drink salt
to gulp air
to wish you were dead
washed ashore
to be glad
thoughts in your head
are only thoughts
in your head.

OF FLESH

Bound to chains of flesh
I crawl the earth
cast upon seeds of grief
for I cannot fly
cannot see beyond
my shadow
am forced to trust
you will return
over and over
to find me
not gone
not buried
not spent
or misplaced
yet born
sworn
forever
to you.

PASSAGE

A passage of dream
eclipse my thinking
took me to a place
buried.

There I lived another life
for hours in my night
bed, bunks, cubby holes
flowing water, camping trolls,
passing strangers,
familiar, yet not,
found stones carried
one by one to a wall
built then re-built
to keep out hands
to keep me still
while I climbed
my journey dream
strange yet familiar
until awaken
into my day
strange yet familiar.

PRISON

A prison lives in my mind
remnants of myself none will find.
Any thought or help to set me free,
gone, walls high as clouds
none allowed, not myself,
not my friends, maybe guests
but then, maybe not
barbed and fenced,
enclosed, incased
barren, remote
confused, erased,
without curfew
entangled in sorrow,
possibly retrievable hope
to open the cage
let my cognizance go
mercy of a loving God
who waits in shimmering glow
through the penal hall
toward the sky,
cerulean peace
in triumphs of
woven comfort
bluffs of home.

PRIVILEGE

Privilege
switched hands with
expectations,
gifts
characterized
as required
led to grave
misunderstandings
no one
went
home
happy
everyone
thought they had
been cheated
when cake
was served.

QUIET TREE

By the sea we sat
me and my quiet tree
neither able to
shake the fear
that dug a hole
by our feet,
there we sat
while waves
pounded shore
breathing
nevermore
as I clung
to my quiet tree
my tree and me
and the sea.

SLAIN DREAMS

Thoughts invade my rest,
warriors battle to kill sleep
slumber lay wounded, lost,
like men at war in tattered fields
remains left of injured dreams.

Yet I dream while awake
of mornings new light
of a new day coming
of a God, my God
who knows me
who speaks to my struggle,
who battles with me,
who says, "Do not fear
I fight for your peace
together we'll keep
your howling night
not to trudge deep
but ground the plight
for spring to chorus
into your night."

THE NIGHT IS NOT MY FRIEND

Dark covers my house
curtains closed
lamps off, TV quiet
my head on a pillow
that refuses my head
not soft, not hard, and not just right
quiet buzzes like sound
infuses air with void,
night cradles my mind
not for slumber,
but for company
while it runs through
details of hours past
dead pets, old shoes, lost jewelry
not calling my mom,
not hugging my son when he was ten,
he still needed hugs,
he seemed so old
how many years
have I left to live,
night keeps me awake
keeps me from sleep,
assumes, I stay awake
as though I could help the dark

the night is not my friend
we battle for sleep,
sleep that yearns
in tender care
the night is not my friend
but arrives and waits
to keep it company.

WE LOVE

We love together
we fight together and lose
let's win, never fight again.

WE SHOULD NOT TALK

We should not talk
let's not say words
even the mention
destroys the good

let's jump in the ocean
drift on rogue waves
until we sink
away, away

at bay to stay
deep in sea
until hurt words
agree to flee.

WHAT BECOMES OF

What becomes of
the laughing baby
the loving hug
the hand reaching for yours
the day he started school
anguish felt to let him go
what becomes of
the bicycle bought for him to ride
picture books bought to shape his life
his jeans, his sweats, his hand made cards
what becomes of
his schoolwork
his education
his guitar
the red tie he worn to the Cotillion
his hair dyed blond
condoms stolen from the Navy Exchange
new beginnings
the fighting
the master's degree
ping pong and popsicles
card games, board games
chess games he lost interest in
what becomes of our worries, our fears,
of never getting there,

ashes.

WISH

An angel alight
upon my wings
lifted my feathers,
soared me to heaven
on a cloud of brush
from hearts of gold
in my daze,
silence arranged a wish,
with twinkling trestles
above fog and sea
a sunlit chiseled road
to go, to be no more,
until God restore
fragmented steps
the garbage dump
of lost ideas and plans
to rise from nothing
from nothing grow.

WONDERFUL MOMENTS

Wonderful moments
fleeting
like air in our lungs
fresh, good, nice
then gone
left behind
crumbs
of loss
that quail

good moments
fleeting, a breeze
to cool ugly truths
that suffocate

good moments
peak into our soul
to let us know
God's goodness reigns
you are not an orphan,
His love remains.

WRITING

My writing was born
unknown, as a child
in continuous words that
played until stories heard,
blurted to my father who listen
as though he cared. He cared.
Planted deeply an invisible seed
in attending to words of a child.

YOUR GRACE

By your grace
hell broke
all the good eggs
worthy and kind
spill to the floor,
stepped on peace
created our war
by your grace
beauty crumbled in dust
by your grace
children wailed,
frowned in distrust
wretched, deprived
soiled in rejection,
by your grace
travelled to hell
lost in dejection

when by your grace
hope broke the fall
filled up the empty
gave courage to crawl
by your grace
melted our hearts
gave solace to lost
gave grace a new start
horrid forgiven
hearts bloomed in kind
in grace we found solace
to retrieve a new mind.

YOU WANT THE TRUTH

One only needs to speak
to dispel the truth
myths are formed the moment
our voice is heard
no one hears the same
everyone distorts,
when words are spoken
arguments ensue
inspired by friends, school, and parents,
random speak, often spoken
without knowledge,
ruin our thoughts
as people talk, the myth is born
good, bad, happy, lost, stupid,
sad, smart, convicted, livid, mad or
the dark corner in your room
silence doesn't exist
dirt smells like worms
bubblegum ice cream is the best
Big Foot lives in Michigan
people live in my dream
planted subconsciously
because my brain is
only partially awake, mostly it sleeps
when I need it most
remember, forget
let's meet again
poetry the emotional splatter of humans
trying hard to hold their myths
keep their head
above muck and grid
I like you; I hate you
let's go wherever the road takes us
the yellow brick road where trees talk
and someone wicked watches our every move.

You want the truth, but not really, so you create myths.

DM completed a BFA and MFA in dance from New York University, Tisch School of the Arts. Lived in NYC's East Village for sixteen years as a modern dancer and worked with many talented choreographers and musicians, including notables as Cindy Lauper, Bertram Ross, Rachel Harms, XXY Dance/ Music and Pierce Turner. To support her career, she worked at more than twenty 'money' jobs such as: art gallery assistant, public relations, commercial modeling, floral design, dance instruction, etc.

After a while she long for a dog and backyard, moved out of New York to the Virginia coast where she adopted a dog, worked at the Governor's School of the Arts, and Christian missions, got married, bought a house on an acre, and had two sons.

Her father was loving, kind, funny and a good listener. His enduring patience to hear every song or tale she told as a child encouraged her creativity, also his devout faith was influential. As a teenager she met Jesus who has been with her ever since.

Her mother was originally from Japan, a strong woman who dived into the sea to spear octopus and provide food for her family, who travelled many rivers and muddy shores, made a subliminal mark, deeper than DM will ever know.

DM writes poetry, children's stories, fiction, non-fiction, and screenplays. She is a creative jack-of-all-trades; interested in everything, but mostly the human dilemma of existence especially late at night when the quiet is loud and keeps her awake.

Her poems come from words that arrive unexpectedly, that carry feelings, lift pain, ease anguish, celebrate disappointment, forgave the unforgiveable, burn the wrongs and tell her, everything is okay when left alone with her terrors. Poetry has been a tool to help wade through the quagmire and finish each day, God willing.

www.ingramcontent.com/pod-product-compliance
Lightning Source LLC
Chambersburg PA
CBHW040308170426
43194CB00022B/2940